Happily Everly After

Written and illustrated by:
Jack & Everly Backe

Everlys Castle

ISBN:
978-1-63308-501-5 (paperback)
978-1-63308-502-2 (ebook)

Interior and Cover Design by *R'tor John D. Maghuyop*
Illustrated by *Jack & Everly Backe*

CHALFANT ECKERT
PUBLISHING

1028 S Bishop Avenue, Dept. 178
Rolla, MO 65401

Printed in United States of America

BOOKS THAT HEAL

presents

Happily Everly After

Written and illustrated by:
Jack & Everly Backe

This book to dedicated to…

This book is dedicated to all the doctors, nurses, clinicians, etc. who have dedicated their lives to working to find a cure for CHD and developing surgeries to help our children with CHD live longer lives.

It is not lost on us that had Everly been born a few decades ago, we would not have even had these two beautiful years with her so far. Because of lots of hard work and research, her prognosis is to live into adulthood.

Thank you!

There are so many people we would like to thank. (And we apologize in advance because we will probably inadvertently forget someone).

We are so incredibly grateful for all of the love and support we've been shown throughout Everly's CHD journey.

We have been showered with support from our amazing family and friends. So many people have come together to make "Everly's village/tribe." The support has helped us through our hardest moments.

A HUGE thank you to Grandma and Grandpa, who we would be lost without. We can't even list all the things they do to keep us going!

Big thank you to Everly and Jack's friends who were guest artists in this book: Briella & Giovanni Buono; Audrey, Brad, & Kara Molter; John, Leo, & Ari Demos; Isabel & Lily Fix; Christian & Cici Carlson; Anders & Mila Martin; Ava & Remy Ganek, and Emma Snodgrass.

Thank you to the Blonskys, the Schebels, and AJ & Sarah, for all their help taking care of Jack on doctor appointment days.

Thank you to Robin Spencer at Scheck & Siress. And the lady at Jobst who made Everly's compression sock kid friendly and a sock for her doll.

Our medical team deserves more appreciation and gratitude than we could possibly put into words. They are absolutely brilliant and also extremely compassionate. Winston Churchill said, *"We make a living by what we get. We make a life by what we give."* It's obvious the clinicians at the Advocate

Heart Institute enjoy giving life to so many children suffering from congenital heart defects. Spend just a few minutes with any of them and you'll quickly see they are experts in all meanings of the word heart, especially the following two: *"a hollow muscular organ that pumps the blood through the circulatory system"* (Google) and also *"the center of the total personality, especially with reference to intuition, feeling, or emotion."* (dictionary.com).

Many, many, many thanks to Everly's very large medical team at Advocate Children's Hospital! (Dr. Ilbawi, Dr. Elzein, Dr. Husayni, Dr. Joshua Wong, Dr. Nater, Dr. Vanbergen, Dr. Roberson, Dr. Sajan, Dr. Hoffman, Dr. Dhaval Patel, Dr. Vicari, Dr. Sherman, Dr. Obringer, Dr. Penk, Dr. Javois, Kelly, Gloria M, Sarah K, Brian H, Tracey O, Chelsea K, Katie W, Jane F, Kelsey S, Katie C, Kate R, Kathleen W, Kyle M, Maggie G, Ashley H, Shannon, Sheila, Jenny, Erin, Jillian B, Anna, Jen F, Melissa M, Carly K, Kristine F, Rachel B, Kristen K, Joan M, Andrea, Diann B, Diane, , Emma, Jean, Lisa, Pammy, Claire, Taz, Megan, Kelsey S, Kathy, Beth, Jenn, Sandy, Maggie, Kim, Rachel, Lindsey, Sarah, Terry, Jackie P, Cindy S, Meg D., Lisa, Jennifer F, Darlene, Maryjane, Joseph…. There are many, many, many more nurses, PCTs, hospital therapists, dieticians, pharmacists & child life specialists that we are so grateful for!)

Many thanks to Everly's local pediatrician- Dr. Mary Collins- and Early Intervention therapy team- Dana, Anne, and Lori!

Thank you to Dr. Randy Wittman, Sandy, and Chrissy who detected Everly's heart defect and help us prepare a team for Everly before her birth.

Thank you to Jack's school and teachers for the enormous amount of support for our family over the past two years! We've been so lucky to have two wonderful teachers supporting Jack since Everly's birth and CHD journey began.

Thank you to photographers: Kristen of Yellow Coat Photography, Bethany of Paint the Sky Photography, Lisa of Photography by Lisa E, and Katie of Kate Hazell Photography for your contributions to this book.

Also, many thanks to the following organizations for helping us throughout our CHD journey: Advocate Children's Heart Institute, The Norwood High Risk Clinic, The Cardiac Neurodevelopment Clinic, The Ronald McDonald House, Starlight Children's Foundation, LJ's Healing Hearts, The Children's Heart Foundation, The Pediatric Congenital Heart Association, The Lemonade Brigade, Brave Gowns, Child Life Mommy, Association for Vascular Access, myIV.com, Mended Little Hearts, The American Heart Association, and AHA: Kids Heart Challenge.

HUGE thank you to Mike Flatley and Books that Heal for this amazing opportunity to share Everly's CHD journey. Our family's hope is that this book will help many other families going through a similar journey to feel less alone. We also hope that all our family, friends, and doctors see how much we appreciate them by reading this story.

And a final thank you to the heart parents who started as strangers and have become friends.

Mommy, Daddy, and my big brother, Jack, couldn't wait to meet me.

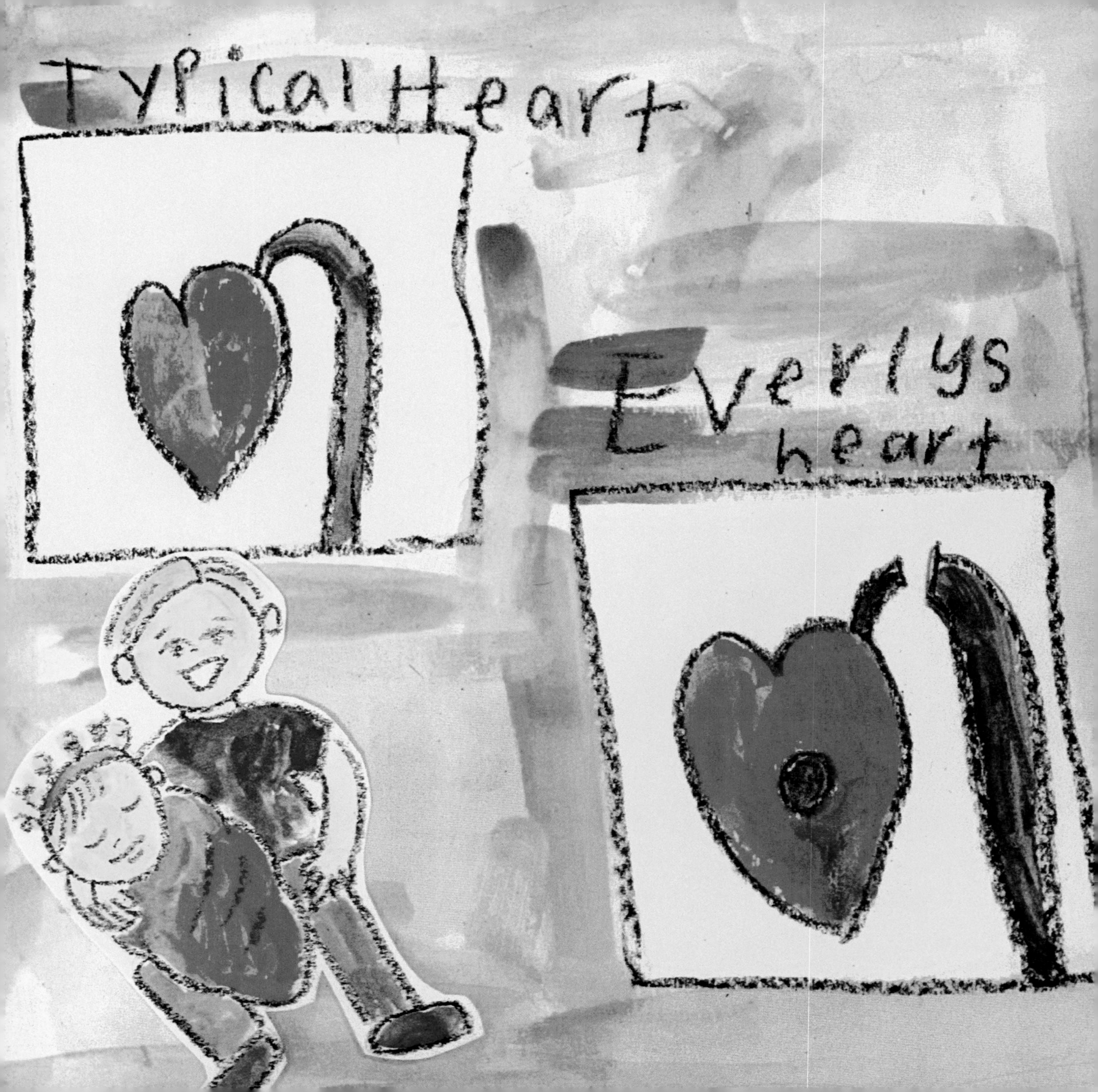
Typical Heart
Everlys heart

They knew my heart was going to need a little extra help when I was born.

I have something called a CHD, congenital heart defect.

Mommy, Daddy, and Jack prepared a special team of all the best doctors and surgeons to take good care of me.

At just 3 days old, I had my first heart surgery. My heart was the size of a walnut. Can you believe my surgeons were mending something so tiny?

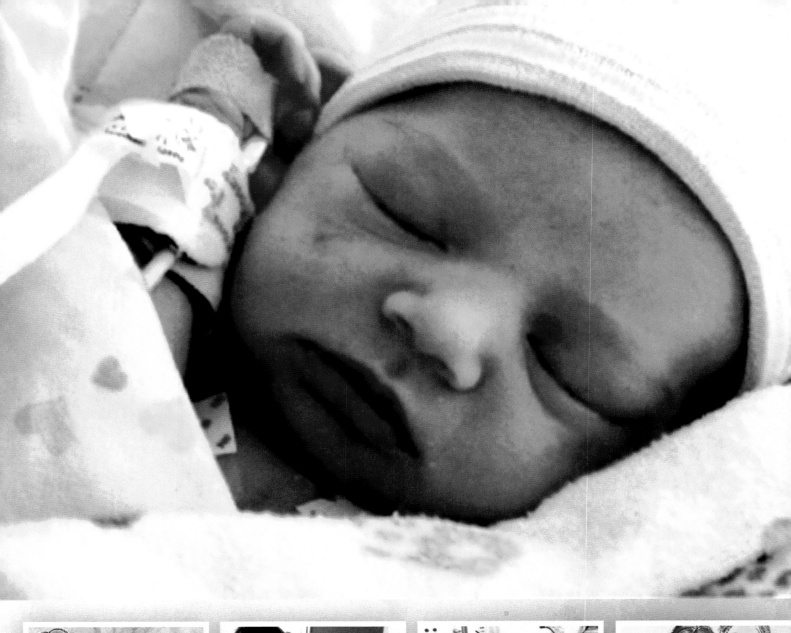

  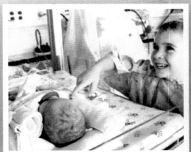 

I did great. That's because
I'm brave and strong.

My family and friends call me a
"heart warrior" because I always impress
everyone with how tough I am.

We were so happy when I finally
got to come home from the hospital.
We could all be together in one place.

My dogs, Maddie and Gracie,
were very excited to meet me.

For a while, I needed some extra help. And people needed to be careful around me so I wouldn't get sick. I had a special straw in my nose to help me drink. And sometimes I needed oxygen to help my heart and lungs. Mommy and

Daddy say they are so grateful for the people who invented all these things. Some days have been hard for me, but I hear my mom say, "You can do anything for a short time" and that helps us get through the tough times.

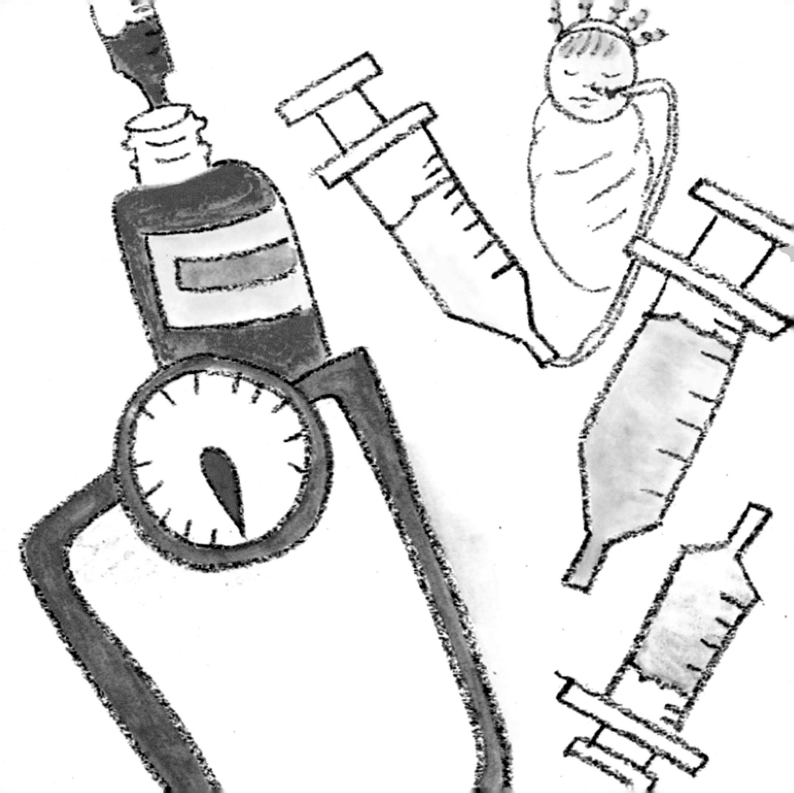

When I was a baby, I needed to be weighed on a special scale every single day to the hundredth of a kilogram.

I had lots of medications to take on a tight schedule all throughout the day. I was a champ at taking my medications to keep my heart safe.

I went to the hospital 60 miles away each Thursday for a very long time. I was part of a high risk clinic because of the type of CHD I have and the type of surgery I had.

Sometimes I wore special monitors at home to send my doctors information about my heart from home. Mommy slept in my room for the first 13 months of my life. It was imperative that I not cry because it would burn too many calories and work my heart too hard.

We always make the best of things.
For the first year of my life, my toes and fingers were always blue because my oxygen levels were a bit different than other people.

So mommy and me had lots of fun painting my nails pink all the time!

DEAR *Santa*
PLEASE FIX MY SISTER'S *heart*
LOVE, *Jack*

Jack is an extra special brother to me.

Do you know what he asked Santa for first thing two years in a row? Right when he sat on Santa's lap, he said,

"Please fix my sister's heart."

Jack also does a great job making sure the windows of my hospital rooms are beautifully decorated.

He gets to use special markers and draw all over for me to see!

Before my third open heart surgery, Jack designed a special, super soft hospital gown for me so I would feel more comfortable. He really is like a knight to me, his princess.

The gown Jack designed for me went out to 30,000 hospitalized kids nationwide, thanks to Starlight Children's Foundation.

The Chicago Cubs were
so proud of Jack, they invited him
and 60 friends to the Cubs game
because they loved his gown.

Lots of Everly's nurses even came to the
game to see Jack! I stayed home with
Grandma and my aunts.

Jack's actually thinking about being a heart doctor….

That is, when he's not also thinking about being a pet doctor or painter or scientist or a YouTube Host/Entrepreneur….

He has plenty of time to decide still….

Princess Everly's VILLAGE

I've had a few more surgeries since that first that when I was just 3 days old. And every time, everyone is so proud of me. I am really awesome. But I'm also really lucky..

People call me "Happily Everly After" and say I'm a princess. I feel like a princess because I've got a knight for a brother. Jack watches out for me and protects me. And I have a whole village of people who care about me: my family, friends, dogs, cardiologists, cardio surgeons, nurses, nurse practitioners, therapists… the list goes on and on.

Ronald McDonald hase

My third open heart surgery was a bit rough on me at the time. But I was lucky Jack came to visit me often and take me for wagon rides around the hospital halls, and sometimes even outside.

Jack stays at Ronald McDonald House with either mommy or daddy when I'm in the hospital. I'm happy I get to have everyone close to me.

You know what's the best wagon ride
when you are in the hospital?
The wagon ride out the door and into
your car to go home!

While we love our hospital
and all the doctors and nurses,
there's no place like home.

I came home from my third open heart surgery just two days before my first birthday. I got to celebrate at home with my family!

I came home with feeding tube in my nose and a PICC line in my arm for IV antibiotics, but I didn't let that stop me from enjoying my first bite of cake!

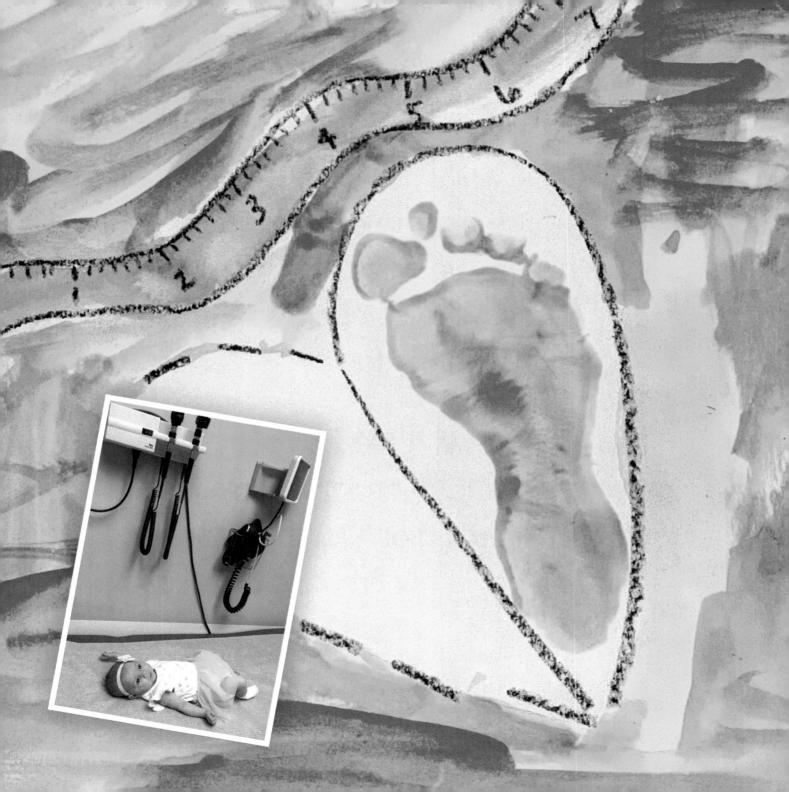

When I was born, it was like I had half a heart. Now the doctors have made my heart whole.

For a while, I was really tiny. I had a hard time growing because my heart was working so hard all the time.

But now I'm growing like a weed!
I'm almost two years old and when
people see me, they have no idea what
I've been through because I'm doing
so well now.

The only way you know I have a CHD is the scar that runs down my chest. I like to think of it as a badge of courage. It's like a medal I wear around with me-- always reminding me just how brave, strong, and tough I am. People say I inspire and impress them.

If you see my scar, it's OK to ask me about it. I'm proud of it. I'm a fighter. I'm a warrior.

I'm just like any other toddler. I don't stop moving. CHD doesn't stop this princess. I run, jump, play, explore. I love to swing, blow bubbles, go for walks with my dogs and dolls, read books, play with our foster puppies, play in the sand….

I love to do really anything my brother is doing. I think I'm 7 just like him.
But my favorite thing to do with him…
is have dance parties in our family room.
Dancing makes everything better!

Do you know what? I've even been feeling so well lately, my family got to go on vacation. We traveled from Chicago to Florida. I loved the beach and pool and warm weather. It was a nice escape from the cold, Chicago winter.

In my first year of life, I was admitted to the hospital 6 times. I had 3 open heart surgeries, 2 cardiac catherizations, and 1 infection wash-out surgery.

Now I'm almost two….and do you know what? I haven't been admitted to the hospital one time in my second year of life. You can tell I'm getting a lot stronger.

Since I've been home more in my second year of life and I've been feeling better, I finally got to meet lots of friends and family.

And friends like Briella, Kara, Cici, Amara, and Emma have been teaching me all about dressing up and how to accessorize!

As I get older, I'll still need my doctors to help my heart. I still have lots of doctor appointments all the time but I'm super lucky. All the clinicians come to visit me when they hear I have an appointment.

Having lots of friends come say hello to me makes the ECHOs, EKGs, x-rays, etc. not so bad, especially when they bring me popsicles! Yum!

There's no cure for CHD right now. But I know some super brilliant people are trying to find one. So for now, there are just fixes, like bandaids. I'll need a few more fixes as I continue to grow. Having more surgeries doesn't sound quite so scary for this princess because I know I'll have my knight, Jack, by my side… along with my village.

You know what my friend Audrey told me the other day? She said, "Everly, I know you are still going to have some scary stuff to go through with CHD, but no matter what, Jack will stay by your side. You know why? Because that's what it means to be a big brother."

Mommy and Daddy say we share my CHD story because we want other CHD families to not feel alone and we want to help make them feel better by hearing how great I'm doing.

My mommy also says,
"Sometimes strength comes in knowing that you aren't alone."

During my first surgery, an IV infiltrated in my foot. It took a really long time for the wound to heal up. Now that foot is still bigger so I wear a special sock to help treat it.

People can really just be so kind. A really nice lady who makes the custom socks bought me a baby doll and made the baby doll a sock that matches mine so we can be twins!

I am doing awesome… I'm living my best life. In our house, we like to think that maybe angels don't just wear wings….

Maybe they wear stethoscopes, scrubs, and special microscope glasses.

We are so thankful for the incredible doctors, surgeons, and nurses who have helped me to live "Happily Everly After."

Made in the USA
Monee, IL
26 March 2022